D0984895

TARANTULAS

Joanne Randolph

PowerKiDS press™

New York

Published in 2014 by The Rosen Publishing Group, Inc.
29 East 21st Street, New York, NY 10010

First Edition

Editor: Jennifer Way and Norman D. Graubart
Book Design: Andrew Povolny
Photo Research: Katie Stryker

Photo Credits: Cover weter 77/Shutterstock.com; pp. 4, 10 Audrey Snider-Bell/Shutterstock.com; p. 5 Lucian Coman/Shutterstock.com; p. 6 Dante Fenolio/Photo Researchers/Getty Images; p. 7 cyrrpit/Shutterstock.com; p. 9 Oxford Scientific/Getty Images; p. 11 (top) Steve Mann/Shutterstock.com; p. 11 (bottom) CraigBurrows/Shutterstock.com; pp. 12–13 Matt Knoth/Shutterstock.com; p. 15 cowboy54/Shutterstock.com; p. 16 TOM MCHUGH/Photo Researchers/Getty Images; p. 17 Dirk Ercken/Shutterstock.com; p. 19 Robert Oelman/Oxford Scientific/Getty Images; p. 20 Kenneth M. Highfill/Photo Researchers/Getty Images; p. 21 CREATISTA/Shutterstock.com; p. 22 Tiburon Studios/E+/Getty Images.

Library of Congress Cataloging-in-Publication Data

Randolph, Joanne.
Tarantulas / by Joanne Randolph.
    pages cm. — (Nightmare creatures–spiders!)
Includes index.
ISBN 978-1-4777-2891-8 (library) — ISBN 978-1-4777-2980-9 (pbk.) —
ISBN 978-1-4777-3050-8 (6-pack)
1. Tarantulas—Juvenile literature. I. Title.
QL458.42.T5R36 2014
595.4'4—dc23
                                2013024245

Manufactured in the United States of America

CPSIA Compliance Information: Batch #W14PK6: For Further Information contact Rosen Publishing, New York, New York at 1-800-237-9932

CONTENTS

Like us on Facebook

MEET THE TARANTULA

When people have nightmares about spiders, the spider they picture is likely the tarantula. Tarantulas are huge and hairy and may look pretty scary. In fact, they are the world's largest spiders.

This is a Goliath bird-eating tarantula. It is the biggest kind of tarantula. It can be 12 inches (30 cm) long!

This tarantula is called a baboon spider. The name comes from the black pads on the ends of its legs that look just like those a baboon has on its feet.

People often have the idea that tarantulas' bites are very **poisonous**, too. It is true that insects usually die from a tarantula bite. Tarantula bites are not harmful to most people, though. The bites hurt, but these spiders have weaker **venom** than a honeybee, so most people have no reaction.

WHERE ARE THE TARANTULAS?

Tarantulas can be found on every **continent** except Antarctica. However, they live mostly in warm places, such as rain forests and deserts. Most tarantula species live in South America.

This tarantula lives in a rain forest. It has used its silk to make a home on top of a leaf.

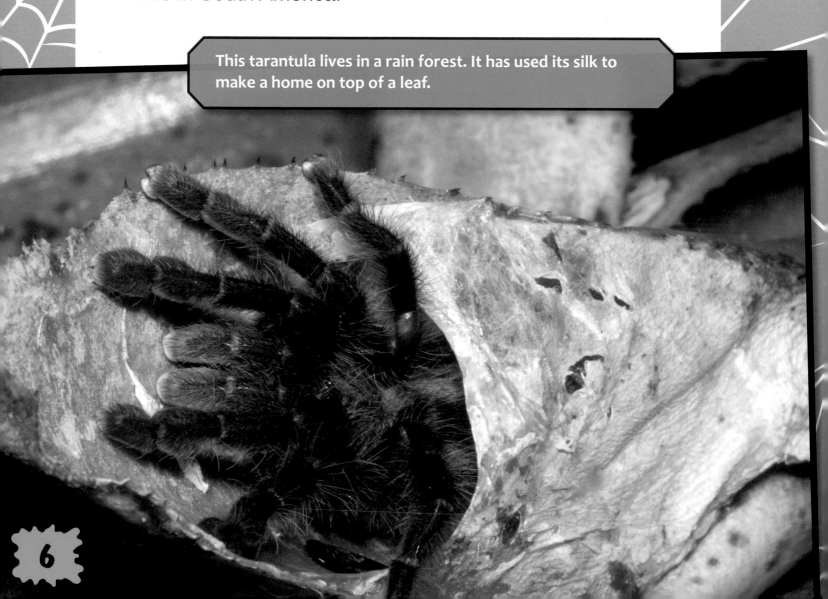

This Mexican red-kneed tarantula has made its home in a cave. It comes out of the cave to catch food, but it can go back into the cave quickly if it senses danger.

Tarantulas that live in deserts are often ground **burrowing**. This means they dig burrows, or holes, in the ground and line them with silk to keep the dirt from caving in. They spend the hot part of the day staying cool in their burrows. Some tarantulas live under rocks or branches on the ground. Other tarantula species make their homes in tree holes.

TARANTULA BODIES

Tarantulas are **arachnids**, as are all other spiders and scorpions. Arachnids have eight legs and two main body parts. The front part is the head. The head is attached to the legs. It also has the eyes and mouthparts. The back part is called the **abdomen**. It has the spinnerets. Spinnerets make silk.

Like all arachnids, tarantulas do not have bones inside their bodies. Instead, they have hard shells on the outsides of their bodies. The shell is called the **exoskeleton**. They must shed their exoskeletons to grow. This is called **molting**. Tarantulas molt many times in their lives to reach their large size.

When tarantulas molt, they lie on their backs on silk mats. Baby tarantulas molt several times each year.

HAIRY SPIDERS

Most tarantulas are very hairy. Some of these hairs are not just for show. Tarantulas have special hairs called urticating, or irritating, hairs. They throw these hairs at animals that enter their territories. Some species of tarantulas use their legs to kick these hairs at their enemies. Others simply wait until an animal brushes against them. If you see a tarantula with a bald spot on its back, it has recently thrown its urticating hairs.

Here you can see the urticating hairs on a Chaco golden knee tarantula.

These special hairs can kill some small animals. For most animals, though, they just cause pain. If a tarantula throws these hairs at a human, it can cause an allergic reaction that can last for a few days.

Some plants have urticating hairs, just like tarantulas! Plants' urticating hairs are often called nettles.

Antilles pinktoe tarantulas are born with blue hair. As they grow, their hair becomes pink, red, and green.

NIGHTMARE FACTS

1. The tarantula's fangs fold back into its mouth like a pocketknife when they are not being used to bite.

2. Goliath bird-eating tarantulas in captivity are usually fed cockroaches.

3. Some tarantulas can live for two years without eating.

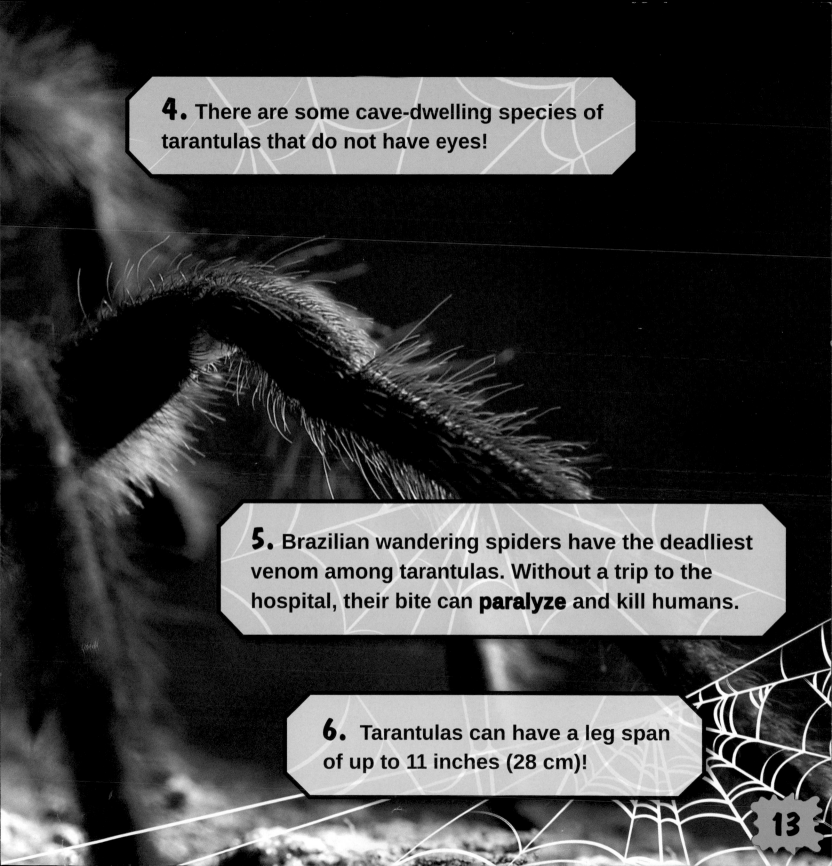

4. There are some cave-dwelling species of tarantulas that do not have eyes!

5. Brazilian wandering spiders have the deadliest venom among tarantulas. Without a trip to the hospital, their bite can **paralyze** and kill humans.

6. Tarantulas can have a leg span of up to 11 inches (28 cm)!

Tarantulas are solitary spiders. This means they spend most of their time alone. They come together only when they are ready to **mate**.

Males are generally smaller than female tarantulas. Males do not live as long either. They do not usually live for more than 2 years after they become full-grown. Some males take only 2 years to grow up, while others take 10 years. Females, on the other hand, continue to eat, grow, and **reproduce** longer than males do. Female tarantulas can sometimes live for up to 40 years.

This is a female giant white knee tarantula in Brazil. Female tarantulas have larger abdomens than male tarantulas. They are more brightly colored.

Tarantulas are hunters, as are all other spiders. They eat mainly insects and other similar animals. The largest tarantulas may eat larger prey. These animals might include mice, lizards, birds, and small snakes.

This tarantula is eating a green-spotted racer snake. This snake is 40 inches (102 cm) long. That's four times the size of the biggest kind of tarantula!

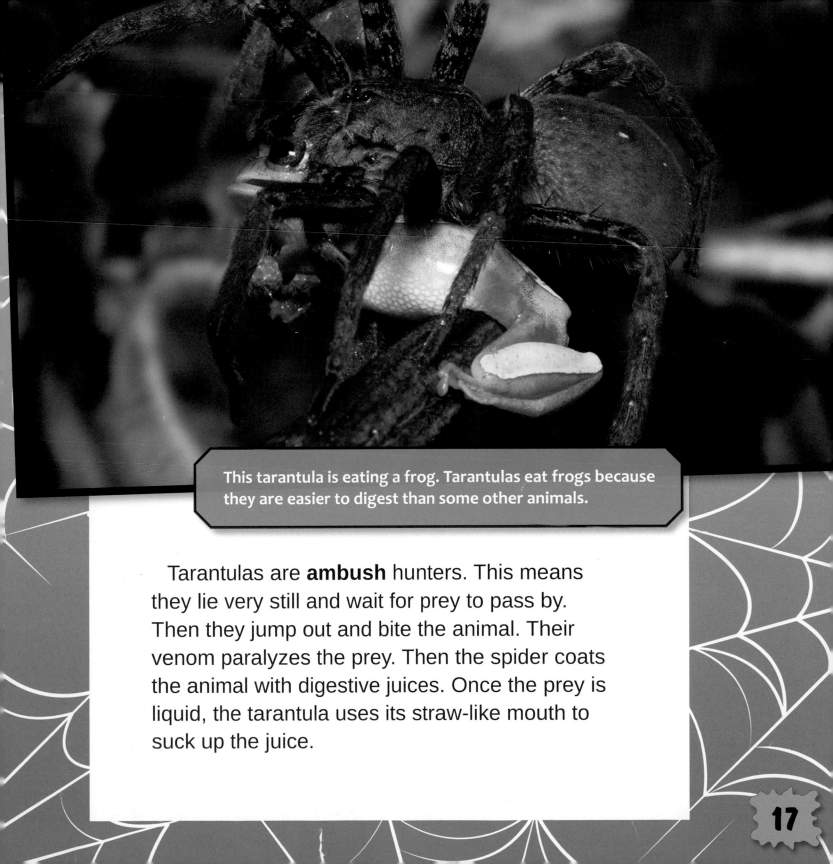

This tarantula is eating a frog. Tarantulas eat frogs because they are easier to digest than some other animals.

Tarantulas are **ambush** hunters. This means they lie very still and wait for prey to pass by. Then they jump out and bite the animal. Their venom paralyzes the prey. Then the spider coats the animal with digestive juices. Once the prey is liquid, the tarantula uses its straw-like mouth to suck up the juice.

WATCH OUT, TARANTULA!

The tarantula's main predator is the tarantula hawk. This is actually a kind of **parasitic** wasp. These wasps will track down tarantulas and then kill them. They stab tarantulas with their stingers in the thinner skin by the spiders' leg joints. This paralyzes the spider. The wasp then drags the spider back to its nest and lays an egg on its abdomen. When the larva hatches, it eats the tarantula.

Many other animals prey on tarantulas, too, including rodents, birds, insects, and even people. Some people in South America and Asia roast the spiders and eat them as a special treat.

This picture shows a tarantula hawk. It is one of the largest types of wasps, but it is smaller than the tarantulas it kills.

BABY TARANTULAS

In each birth cycle, females lay 100 to 1,000 eggs and seal them inside egg sacs made from silk. The female tarantula watches the sac closely and turns it every now and then. When the baby tarantulas are ready, they break free from their eggs and then the sac. Once they hatch, they are on their own.

Here is a newly hatched Texas brown tarantula sitting on its mother's leg.

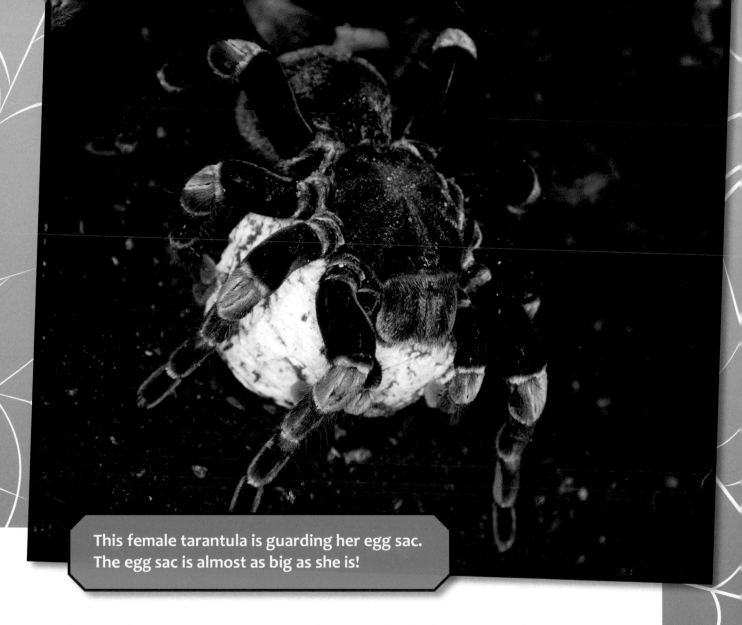

This female tarantula is guarding her egg sac. The egg sac is almost as big as she is!

As the baby spiders grow, they molt. Before tarantulas molt, they stop eating and do not move much for a few days. After molting, they spend another few days not eating as they wait for their fangs and exoskeleton to harden.

TARANTULAS AND PEOPLE

Many people are scared of all kinds of spiders. To these people, tarantulas must seem like the scariest. However, tarantulas, and all spiders, are important and helpful creatures. They eat lots of bugs that are harmful to humans and crops.

Some people keep these spiders as pets. Even if a huge, hairy spider does not seem like a good pet to you, hopefully you have learned what makes tarantulas some of the most interesting spiders.

An adult is helping a kid hold a tarantula at a science museum. If you want to handle a tarantula, always ask an adult first.

GLOSSARY

abdomen (AB-duh-mun) The large, rear part of an arachnid's body.

ambush (AM-bush) A surprise attack.

arachnids (uh-RAK-nidz) A type of animal, such as spiders, scorpions, or ticks.

burrowing (BUR-oh-ing) Digging a hole in the ground for shelter.

continent (KON-tuh-nent) One of Earth's seven large landmasses.

exoskeleton (ek-soh-SKEH-leh-tun) The hard covering on the outside of an animal's body that holds and guards the soft insides.

mate (MAYT) To come together to make babies.

molting (MOHLT-ing) Shedding hair, feathers, shell, horns, or skin.

paralyze (PER-uh-lyz) To take away feeling or movement.

parasitic (per-uh-SIH-tik) Having to do with a living thing that lives in, on, or with another living thing.

poisonous (POYZ-nus) Causing pain or death with matter made by an animal's body.

reproduce (ree-pruh-DOOS) To have babies.

venom (VEH-num) A poison passed by one animal into another through a bite or a sting.

INDEX

WEBSITES

Due to the changing nature of Internet links, PowerKids Press has developed an online list of websites related to the subject of this book. This site is updated regularly. Please use this link to access the list: www.powerkidslinks.com/ncs/tarant/